AL PACKER

lorado Cannibal

Fred and Jo Mazzulla

Maybe Packer was Republican,

    But there's no room for doubt

His mistake was "eatin' Dimmycrats."

    Now we just chew 'em out.

                            —Gene Lindberg

AL PACKER

A Colorado Cannibal

●

Colorado

Cannibal

Consumes and

Cashes in on

Companions

Fred and Jo Mazzulla

Packer Diorama in the
Denver Historical Wax Museum

THE STATE OF COLORADO
EXECUTIVE CHAMBERS
DENVER

JOHN A. LOVE
GOVERNOR

The Old West was seldom quiet, sometimes harsh, often brutal, many times shocking, always exciting. The settling of the West is a spectacular chapter in the growth of our country.

One of the bizarre stories of this period is the tale of Alferd Packer, the Colorado prospector. Beset by the cold, starvation, and physical and mental suffering beyond belief, Packer is alleged to have killed five of his fellow prospectors and lived off their flesh.

The trail up "Slum Gullion Pass" to "Cannibal Plateau" is still visited by tourists who have a "moth and flame" desire to see the site of this tragic happening.

The story of Alferd Packer is not a pretty one, but it is a part of the heritage of Colorado and the West. The authors of this book are master story tellers, and their extensive research gives perspective insight into the human elements of this tragedy.

John a Love
John A. Love

3

CHRONOLOGY

Jan. 21, 1842 — Alferd Packer born in Allegheny Co., Pa.

April 22, 1862 — Enlisted in Union Army at Winona, Minnesota.

Dec. 29, 1862 — Honorable disability discharge at Fort Ontario, N.Y.

Nov. 8, 1873 — Party of 21 left Bingham Canyon, Utah.

Jan. 21, 1874 — Party arrived at Ouray's Camp.

Feb. 9, 1874 — Party of 6 left Ouray's Camp.

April 16, 1874 — Packer arrived at Los Pinos Agency.

May 8, 1874 — "1st" confession to General Adams.

Aug. 8, 1874 — Packer escaped from Saguache dungeon jail.

March 11, 1883 — Packer arrested near Fort Fetterman, Wyoming.

March 16, 1883 — Packer made 2nd confession at Denver, Colorado.

April 6-13, 1883 — 1st trial at Lake City, Colorado — Death Penalty.

May 19, 1883 — Scheduled date of Execution.

Oct. 30, 1885 — Conviction reversed. Death Penalty vacated.

Apr. 15, 1883-Aug. 5, 1886 — Packer in Gunnison, Colorado jail.

Aug. 2-5, 1886 — 2nd trial at Gunnison, Colo. — 40 years.

Aug. 6, 1886-Jan. 10, 1901 — In Colorado penitentiary.

Jan. 10, 1901 — Packer paroled by Gov. Thomas.

April 19-28, 1900 — 1st trial of "Plug Hat" — Hung jury.

Aug. 2-11, 1901 — 2nd trial of "Plug Hat" — Hung jury.

Nov. 12-16, 1901 — 3rd trial of "Plug Hat" — Not guilty.

April 23, 1907 — Packer died — buried in Littleton, Colorado.

Oct. 27, 1907 — Expiration date of Alferd Packer's Parole.

UTE CHIEF OURAY

The Packer "21" party
arrived at his Winter Camp
on Jan. 21, 1874.

OTTO MEARS

The pathfinder of the San
Juans — Soldier — Indian
Agent — Transportation
Tycoon — Publisher —
Builder. He played a leading
role in the Packer Story.
He was under-educated
and under-privileged.

ALFERD PACKER
Colorado Cannibal

Alferd Packer, a Cannibal, was born in Allegheny County, Pa., January 21, 1842. He was by occupation, a shoemaker. At the age of 20, he enlisted in the Union Army, April 22, 1862, at Winona, Minnesota, and was honorably discharged December 29, 1862, at Fort Ontario, New York, due to disability. He went west working at his trade and engaged in prospecting.

On November 8, 1873, as a guide for a party of 21 men, he left Bingham Canyon, Utah to go to the gold fields of Colorado Territory. Part of their food supply was accidentally lost crossing a river on a raft. A most severe winter made travel extremely hazardous. The food ran out. Late in January of 1874 they found shelter and food at Chief Ouray's camp near Montrose, Colorado. On February 9th, Packer and five companions left the camp, contrary to the advice of Ouray.

Packer arrived alone at the Los Pinos Indian Agency, near Saguache, on April 16, 1874. He was fat and had plenty of money. His conduct invited suspicion and questioning by Otto Mears and General Adams. Packer broke down and made two confessions. He admitted that he had lived off of the flesh of his five companions the bigger part of the sixty days he was lost between Lake San Cristobal and Los Pinos Agency.

The five bodies were found. Packer was placed in a dungeon in Saguache, but made good his escape through the aid of an accomplice on August 8, 1874. He was arrested eight years later near Fort Fetterman, Wyoming, March 11, 1883. He was tried at Lake City, Colorado, April 6-13, 1883, found guilty and sentenced to death.

The Lynch Mob was ready to take over. To prevent this, Packer was moved during the night to the Gunnison jail, where he remained for three years. His case was appealed to the Colorado Supreme Court and reversed on October 30, 1885 (8 Colo. 361, 8 Pac. 564) due to a technicality, because he was charged under a Territorial law, but tried under a State law. The second trial was held in Gunnison, Colorado, August 2-5, 1886. The jury returned a verdict of guilty of manslaughter for each of the five victims. The court sentenced the defendant to 8 years for each of the 5 victims, or a total of 40 years.

Packer served in the penitentiary at Canon City, Colorado from 1886 to 1901.

Sob sister Polly Pry of *The Denver Post,* and lawyer Wm. W. "Plug Hat" Anderson were given the task of getting Packer paroled. "Plug Hat" came up with the proposition that the offense having occurred on an Indian Reservation, the trial should have been in a Federal court and not a State court. There appears to be merit to this theory.

Bonfils and Tammen wanted Packer as a sideshow freak with their Sells-Floto Circus. Governor Thomas sent to Salt Lake City for Doc Shores. Doc told of intercepting Packer's mail while he was sheriff of Gunnison County. Doc testified that Al was filthy, vulgar, selfish, and to sum up, a disgrace to the human race. *The Post* was winning the fight, but the Governor had an ace up his sleeve. On January 10, 1901, Packer signed a parole agreement that provided, "He (Packer) shall proceed at once to Denver, and there remain, if practicable, for a period of at least six years and nine months from this date."

Packer had earned about $1,500.00 making hair rope and hair bridles while a prisoner. He paid "Plug Hat" a fee of $25.00. Bon and Tam demanded half of the fee. An argument developed in Bonfils' office. Present were Bonfils, Tammen, Polly Pry and Anderson. Bonfils struck Anderson across the face. Anderson went across the street, got his gun and returned to the office, entered without knocking and shot Bonfils in the neck and chest and Tammen in the shoulder and chest. Both ducked under Polly's full skirt. Anderson had fired four times and had one shot left in his gun. He was waiting to use that last bullet. Bonfils raised Polly's skirt to see what was going on. Anderson noticed that Bonfils was shaking like a leaf and that he was dripping wet. This struck Anderson's funny bone, and he jumped up and down and rocked with laughter. That laughter saved the lives of the owners of *The Post.*

Anderson was tried three times for the crime of assault with the intent to murder. The first trial started April 19, 1900 and lasted 9 days. The jury disagreed and was discharged. The same result was produced after a 9-day trial on August 2, 1901. The third trial started November 12, 1901, and four days later the jury returned a verdict of "not guilty."

The defense attorney, Col. John G. Taylor, made this statement, "I believe that *The Denver Times* was fairer to us than any other paper. The tone all the way through showed the facts exactly as they were, and I desire to give due credit to the stand the paper took in the matter."

The trial judge said to Anderson: "Your motive was admirable, but your marksmanship was abominable."

The Packer Story was popularized by Gene Fowler, Ralph Carr, and Herndon Davis. Our Colorado Cannibal is hashed and rehashed badly by pulp magazines at least twice a year. We know this to be true because we sell them the pictures. Members of The Packer Club can be found in all parts of the world. Today, you can buy a Packer sandwich and a membership card in The Packer Club for $1.50.

Packer died April 23, 1907 and is buried in Littleton, Colorado. Thousands of tourists visit his grave every summer.

Ralph Carr

Gene Fowler

Herndon Davis

HUMAN JERKED BEEF.

The Man Who Lived on Meat Cut From His Murdered Victims.

The Fiend Who Became Very Corpulent Upon a Diet of Human Steaks.

A Cannibal Who Gnaws on the Choice Cuts of His Fellow-Man.

Packer Arrives in Denver and Meets and Recognizes General Adams.

He Makes a Confession, But Studiously Ignores the Five-Fold Murder.

He Says He Subsisted For Sixty Days Upon Human Flesh.

Particulars of the Tragedy From Denverites Conversant With the Facts.

it. I tried to get away (so I lived on the flesh o part of the sixty days I began to have a crust a: creek to a place wher come down the moun [slumgullion]; there I s wet, and having only a them I froze my feet ur before I reached the top ing all night; the next d hill and a little over. I log and on two logs clos

COOKED SOME

And carried it with me one blanket. There was fetched it out with me headed man, Bell, had All the others together l myself. If there was an fit I did not know of it a the last camp, just befor ate my last pieces of ine the camp before I started and carried the bag with a little at a time. Whe party from the agency to came to the mountains but I did not want to tai

DID NOT WAN

To the camp. If I ha longer I would have tak right to the place, but ' away. [The prisoner de were.] When I was at the She I was passed a key made with which I could unlc the Arkansas and worl Gill, eighteen miles belo Gilbert's ranch, still far in a crop of corn, sold I to Arizona. (Signed) STATE OF COLORADO, } County of Arapahoe. } I, Al. Packer, of my rily do swear that the ab whole truth and nothing

Subscribed t day of March.

T The swo differs very Packer at t Ute agency. lows: When the s:

Denver
Republican
3-17-83

Gunnison Daily
Review Press
5-12-83

NNISON, COLORADO, SAT

THE MURDERERS' MIRTH

The Supreme Court Says Murder is not a Crime

If Committed Previous to the 28th Day of May, 1881.

Packer will not Hang May 19th, as Ordered.

Packer Free.

Special to Daily-Review Press.

DENVER, Colo., May 11.—The Supreme Court reversed the decision in the Garvey case this morning. It holds that Garvey cannot be tried for murder. This will affect the Packer and also the Brennen case from Gunnison.

Con Th nigh pass spel tract At a Fish for "bei form ty p equs pers eral pick be " was tion phs' PRE

There were two Los Pinos Agencies — The *old* and the *new*. This rare photo of the *old* near Cochetopa was taken in 1875.

Ute Chief Tapuche   Chief Ouray   George Beckwith

1878 Photo of the *new* Los Pinos Agency

THE PACKER CASE.

Trial of the Man Eater For Manslaughter Begun.

Interesting History of the Crime and Details of Previous Trial.

The Finding of the Bodies of his Five Victims.

The Horrible Story Told By the Survivors After Twelve Years.

The trial of Alfred Packer, charged with manslaughter, in having on or about March 19, 1874 killed Israel Swan, Shannon Wilson Bell, Frank Miller, George Noon and James Humphrey, now before the court is one of unusual interest.

Packer was arraigned Saturday, before Judge Harrison. District Attorney H. M. Hogg, assisted by J. W. Mills Esq. of Hins-

San Cristoba
stands, and
five men.
Saguache b
been held th
had escaped.
water countr
1882-3, was
Hinsdale cou
the revival o
immense exc
Five indict
man killed, v
Hinsdale cou
then and the
ment—the k
guilty and s
hanged. U
court the dec
a former wel
declaring the
operative as t
a bungling le
to amend, re
act.
The case w
upon the char
crime punishe
two years ela
decision was
has been in tl
by Hinsdale c
thi
bi
ha
na
da

Gunnison
Review Press
8-3-86

PACKER'S STATEMENT.

Put Upon the Stand He Tells His Own Story.

In Self Defense He Killed Bell, Who Tried to Kill Him.

Prognostications About the Next Presidential Campaign.

Governor Ireland, of Texas, on the War Path Against Mexico.

The Packer Trial.

The prosecution in the Packer case closed its testimony at 9:30 this a. m., and the defense immediately put Packer on the stand to testify in his own behalf.

No pen can do justice to a report of Packer's statement, which was so rambling, many times incoherent, and at all times so disjointed that only a stenographer could follow him. He attempted to give a history of his

ASPE

A Compa
Causes of
ing for
Lines—Tl

ASPEN, C
just now wo
with the fac
a year ag
Leadville.
there were t
there is but
few hundred
evening ther
four thousan
promising to
Aspen in 18
erate on the
ing propertie
not to excee
ployed on an

You ask v
the mines
mining boom
tions and sal
Twelve mont
went through
Then I wrote
predicted the
exists to-day.
I have freque
Aspen people
son familiar v
towns could r
the line in wl

Gunnison
Review Press
8-2-86

11

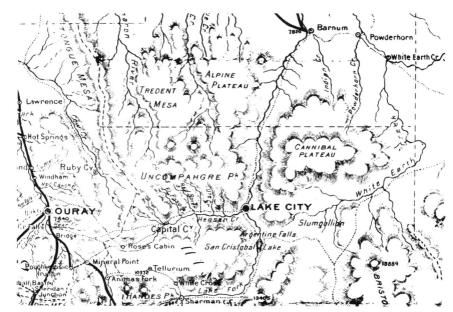

Cannibal Plateau

Sketch made by John A. Randolph of the victims.
From Harper's Weekly, October 17, 1874.

Lake City, Colo., Court House, built in 1877, in foreground.

Lake City Courthouse — 1953 photo.

13

Packer was tried in this second story courtroom in Lake City courthouse April 6-13, 1883, and found guilty of murder by the jury.

The trial of Packer as painted by noted artist, Herndon Davis. His best known work is "The Face on the Floor" in Central City, Colo.

Judge M. B. Gerry presided at the Lake City trial of Packer. He was born in Florida, and died Feb. 17, 1912 at Biloxi, Mississippi, at the age of 72. He left Colorado in 1902 to make his home in Rome, Georgia. He is buried in Macon, Georgia.

15

District Attorney John C. Bell prosecuted Packer in the Lake City Trial.

J. Warner Mills was the assistant District Attorney at both the Lake City trial and at the Gunnison trial of Packer.

ALFERD
PACKER

Our Colorado Cannibal was
born in Allegheny Co., Pa. 21
January 1842. A shoemaker
by profession, he enlisted in the
Union Army from Winona,
Minn. 22 April 1862 for a 3
year hitch; and was assigned to
the 16 Inf. Regiment. Due to
a disability, he was discharged
at Ft. Ontario, N.Y., as a re-
cruit on Dec. 29, 1862 with a
25.00 monthly pension. He
died near Littleton, Colorado
April 23, 1907.

HINSDALE COUNTY
LAKE CITY, COLORADO

THE SENTENCE OF ALFRED PACKER BY
JUDGE M. B. GERRY

COPIED FROM THE
DISTRICT COURT RECORDS

"It becomes my duty as the Judge of this Court to enforce the verdict of the jury rendered in your case, and impose on you the judgment which the law fixes as the punishment of the crime you have committed. It is a solemn, painful duty to perform. I would to God the cup might pass from me. You have had a fair and impartial trial. You have been faithfully and earnestly defended by able Counsel. The presiding judge of this court upon his oath and his conscience, has labored to be honest and impartial in the trial of your case and in all doubtful questions presented you have had the benefit of the doubt.

"A jury of twelve honest citizens of the County have sat in judgment on your case and upon their oaths they find you guilty of wilful and premeditated murder — a murder revolting in all its details. In 1874 you, in company with five companions, passed through this beautiful mountain valley where stands the town of Lake City. At that time the hand of man had not marred the beauties of nature. The picture was fresh from the hand of the Great Artist who created it. You and your companions camped at the base of a grand old mountain, in sight of the place you now stand, on the banks of a stream as pure and beautiful as ever traced by the finger of God upon the bosom of earth. Your very surrounding was calculated to impress upon your heart and nature the omnipotence of Deity and the helplessness of your own feeble life. In this goodly favored spot you conceived your murderous designs.

18

"You and your victims had had a weary march, and when the shadows of the mountains fell upon your little party and night drew her sable curtain around you, your unsuspecting victims lay down on the ground and were soon lost in the sleep of the weary; and when thus sweetly unconscious of danger from any quarter, and particularly from you, their trusted companion, you cruelly and brutally slew them all. Whether your murderous hand was guided by the misty light of the moon, or the flickering blaze of the camp fire, you can only tell. No eye saw the bloody deed performed; no ear, save your own, caught the groans of your dying victims. You then and there robbed the living of life, and then robbed the dead of the reward of honest toil which they had accumulated; at least so say the jury.

"To other sickening details of your crime I will not refer. Silence is kindness. I do not say these things to harrow up your soul, for I know

Draft of the "first" confession in Packer's own handwriting. Made at Los Pinos Agency on May 5, 1874.

you have drunk the cup of bitterness to its very dregs, and wherever you have gone the stings of your conscience and the goadings of remorse have been an avenging Nemesis which has followed you at every turn in life and pained afresh for your contemplation the picture of the past. I say these things to impress upon your mind the awful solemnity of your situation and the impending doom which you cannot avert. Be not deceived. God is not mocked, for whatsoever a man soweth, that shall he also reap. You, Alfred Packer, sowed the wind; you must now reap the whirlwind. Society cannot forgive you for the crime you have committed; it enforces the Old Mosaic law of a life for a life, and your life must be taken as the penalty of your crime. I am but the instrument of society to impose the punishment which the law provides. While society cannot forgive, it will forget. As the days come and go and the years of your pilgrimage roll by, the memory of you and of your crimes will fade from the minds of men.

"With God it is different. He will not forget, but will forgive. He pardoned the thief on the Cross. He is the same God today as then — A God of love and mercy, of long-suffering and kind forbearance; A God who tempers the wind to the shorn lamb, and promises rest to all the weary and heartbroken children of men; and it is to this God I commend you.

"Close your ears to the blandishments of hope. Listen not to its fluttering promises of life. But prepare to meet the spirits of thy murdered victims. Prepare for the dread certainty of death. Prepare to meet thy God; prepare to meet that aged father and mother of whom you have spoken and who still love you as their dear boy.

"For nine long years you have been a wanderer upon the face of the earth, bowed and broken in spirit; no home; no loves; no ties to bind you to earth. You have been, indeed, a poor, pitiful waif of humanity. I hope and pray that in the spirit land to which you are so fast and surely drifting, you will find that peace and rest for your weary spirit which this world cannot give.

"Alfred Packer, the judgment of this Court is that you be removed from thence to the jail of Hinsdale County and there confined until the 19th day of May, A.D. 1883, and that on said 19th day of May, 1883, you be taken from thence by the sheriff of Hinsdale County, to a place of execution prepared for this purpose at some point within the corporate limits of the town of Lake City, in the said County of Hinsdale, and between the hours of 10:00 A.M. and 3:00 P.M. of said day, you, then and there, by said sheriff be hung by the neck until you are dead, dead, dead, and may God have mercy upon your soul!"

Gunnison
Daily Review-Press
April 14, 1883

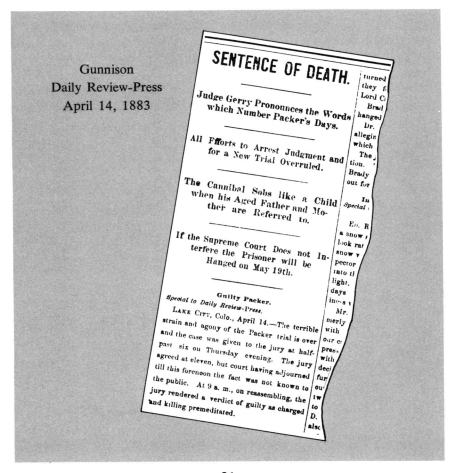

SENTENCE OF DEATH.

Judge Gerry Prononnces the Words which Number Packer's Days.

All Fforts to Arrest Judgment and for a New Trial Overruled.

The Cannibal Sobs like a Child when his Aged Father and Mother are Referred to.

If the Supreme Court Does not Interfere the Prisoner will be Hanged on May 19th.

Guilty Packer.

Special to Daily Review-Press.

LAKE CITY, Colo., April 14.—The terrible strain and agony of the Packer trial is over and the case was given to the jury at half-past six on Thursday evening. The jury agreed at eleven, but court having adjourned till this forenoon the fact was not known to the public. At 9 a. m., on reassembling, the jury rendered a verdict of guilty as charged and killing premeditated.

21

PACKER CLUB

AL PACKER

"They was siven Dimmycrats in Hinsdale County, but you, yah voracious, man-eatin' son of a bitch, yah eat five of thim!"

I agrees to eliminat five Nu Deal Dimmycrats witch makes me a mimber of th' PACKER CLUB of COLORADO

SIGN HERE

_____

26 COLO.306   57 PAC.1087
TIMBER LINE   PAGE 37

Greystone Color

CHARTER MEMBERS: RALPH CARR, GENE FOWLER, HERNDON DAVIS, FRED MAZZULLA

The Packer Club wants more members!

22

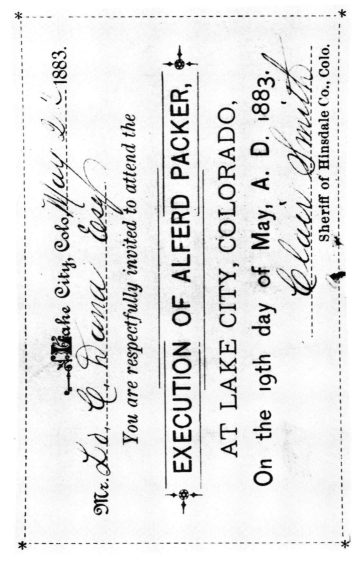

Lake City, Colo. May 2 1883.

Mr. Ed C. Dana Esq.

You are respectfully invited to attend the

★ EXECUTION OF ALFERD PACKER, ★

AT LAKE CITY, COLORADO,

On the 19th day of May, A. D. 1883.

Clair Smith

Sheriff of Hinsdale Co., Colo.

Invitation to Execution. *Note correct spelling of name Alferd.*

23

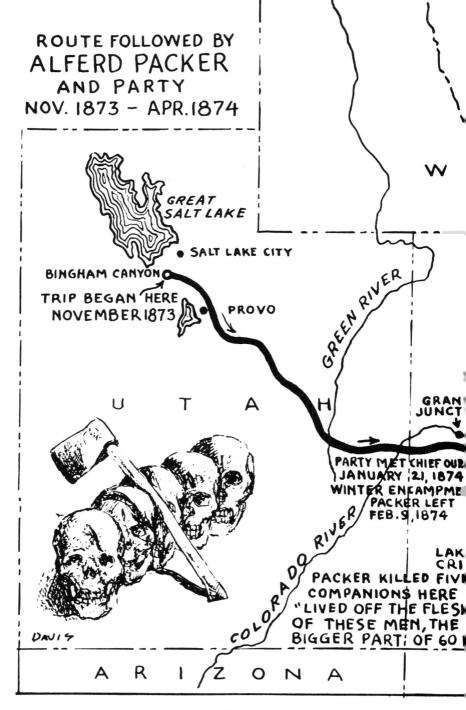

ROUTE FOLLOWED BY
ALFERD PACKER
AND PARTY
NOV. 1873 – APR. 1874

GREAT
SALT LAKE

● SALT LAKE CITY

BINGHAM CANYON ○

TRIP BEGAN HERE
NOVEMBER 1873

● PROVO

GREEN RIVER

U T A H

GRAN
JUNCT

PARTY MET CHIEF OUR
JANUARY 21, 1874
WINTER ENCAMPME
PACKER LEFT
FEB. 9, 1874

COLORADO RIVER

LAK
CRI
PACKER KILLED FIVE
COMPANIONS HERE
"LIVED OFF THE FLES
OF THESE MEN, THE
BIGGER PART OF 60

DAVIS

W

A R I Z O N A

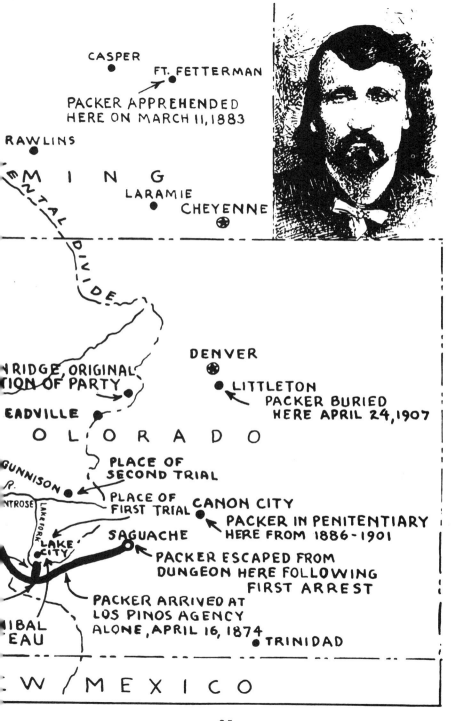

CASPER
●

FT. FETTERMAN
●

PACKER APPREHENDED
HERE ON MARCH 11, 1883

RAWLINS
●

EMING

LARAMIE
●

CHEYENNE
⊛

ENTAL DIVIDE

DENVER
⊛

NRIDGE, ORIGINAL
TION OF PARTY
●

LITTLETON
●
PACKER BURIED
HERE APRIL 24, 1907

EADVILLE
●

OLORADO

GUNNISON
R.
●

PLACE OF
SECOND TRIAL

NTROSE

PLACE OF
FIRST TRIAL

CANON CITY
●
PACKER IN PENITENTIARY
HERE FROM 1886-1901

LAKEFORK

SAGUACHE

LAKE
CITY
●

PACKER ESCAPED FROM
DUNGEON HERE FOLLOWING
FIRST ARREST

PACKER ARRIVED AT
LOS PINOS AGENCY
ALONE, APRIL 16, 1874

TRINIDAD
●

IBAL
EAU

W / MEXICO

GUNNISON IN 1886

Herschel Millard Hogg
District Attorney who
prosecuted Packer in the
2nd trial at Gunnison, Colo.,
Aug. 2-5, 1886.

Sheriff Cyrus W. "Doc" Shores and Mrs. Shores lived in this house facing the D. & R.G. R.R. at the rear of the La Veta Hotel in Gunnison. Note Masonic Pin on Mrs. Shores. 1883 Photo.

I Alfred Packer desire to make a true and voluntary statement in regard to the occurrences in Southern Colorado during the winter 1873 – 1874. I wish to make it to [Wm.] Statement because I have made one once before about the same matter. —

When we left Ouray's camp we had about 7 days feed for one man, we traveled two or 3 days and it came a storm we came to a mountain, covered

a stream, which runs into a
big Lake, the second time
just above the Lake. - The
next morning we crossed the lake
cut holes into the ice to catch
fish, there were as fast as we
tried to catch it, snails, the
ice was thin, some broke through
We crossed the lake and went
into a grove of timber, see
The men crying and one of
them was crazy. - Snow asked
to go and could see something
one whether I could see something
from the mountains - I took
a gun went up the hill, found

a quick aid came into another
mountain found the snow
so deep, had to follow the
mountain. On the top and on
about the 4th day we had about
a foot of snow left; We
followed the mountain until
we came to the main range
we can not remember how many
days we were traveling then -
about 10 days - living on rosebuds
and pine gum and some of
the men were crying and crazy
Then we came over the main
range we camped twice on

29

The hatchet off from the fire (down the stream, his face was crushed in with the hatchet. The other three men were lying near the fire, they were cut in the forehead with the hatchet some had two some three cuts – I came within a rod of the fire, when the man saw me he got up with his hatchet toward me when I shot him sideways through the belly he fell on his face. The hatchet fell from his face. The hatchet fell from I grabbed it and him in the

a big notebook and had a through the snow, but could see nothing but snow all around. I was a kind of a guide for them but I did not know the mountains from that side. When I came back to camp after being gone nearly all day I found the unheated man who acted crazy in the (Busy) morning sitting near the fire. roasting a piece of meat which he had cut out of the leg of the German butcher (Muller) the calves body was lying

30

camp. The piece of meat that was near the fire. — I made a new fire near my camp and cooked the piece of meat and ate it. — I tried to get away every day but could not as I lived off the flesh of these oxen, the bigger part of the 60 days I was sick. — Then the snow began to have a crust and I started out up the creek to a place where a big slide seemed to come down the mountain of yellowish clay

I camped that night at the fire, lit up all night. The next morning I followed up the mountain my tracks, but I could not make it, the snow was too deep and I came back, I went sideways into a piece of pine timber set up two sticks and covered it with pine boughs and then made a shelter about 3 feet high, then was my camp until I came out. — I went back to the fire carried the meat up and fetched to the

31

There was seventy Dreem amongst the men I fetched it out with me and one gun. The redeemed man had 30 Dreem Bee in his pocket and 30 Dreem [?] had only 20 Dollar all. The others [?] had only 20 Dollars.

I had 20 Dreem my self. If there was any more money in the outfit, I did not know of it and it remained there. All the had camp just before I reached the agency I ate my last piece of meat. Then meat I cooked & the camp before I started out and I carried only one blanket

& there I started up - but got my feet wet and having only a piece of blanket around them. Then I froze my first [?] night till I reached the top. I camped under the [?] before I reached the top making a fire and stayed all night.

The next day I made the top of the hill and a little over. I built a fire on top of a log - two logs close together and my [?] log and I camped there. - I cooked some of the [?] and carried it with me for food. I carried only one blanket

When I was at the Sheriff
in Saguache I was passed
a key made out of pen
knife blade with which
I could unlock the irons
I went to the Arkansas
and worked all summer
for John Gill 18 miles
below the Pueblo, then
I rented Gilbert ranche
still further down but
in a crop of corn, does it
and went to Arizona, John
Gill bought my corn —

the bag Bill me, I could not
eat but a little at a time.
When I went out with
the party to search for the
bodies, we came to the
mountain overlooking
the stream but I did not
want to take them further
I did not want to go back
to the camp myself. —
If I had still ...
I would have taken you
right to the
(Mrs Adams) but they advised me
to go away (Refusing to tell
the place "
to go away (Refusing to tell
the names of the parties)

I, Alfred Packer, of
my own free will and
voluntarily do swear that
the above statement is
true, the whole truth and
nothing but the truth
So help me God

Alfred Packer

Subscribed and sworn to before
me this 16th day of March A.D. 1883

Sieu W. McCautril
Notary Public

(Seal)

Forest Service Marker at Cannibal Plateau.

The Burial Place for the 5 Victims — Harper's Weekly, 17 Oct. 1874

Packer's
Prison
Picture

Packer's
Prison Record

#1399   A. Packer.

Crime - Manslaughter
Term - 40 years
County - Gunnison

Age - 38   Hair - Chestnut
Hight - 5-10½   Occu - Harness Mkr.
Com - Light   Build - Slender
Eyes - Blue

Marks & Scars

1st & 4th. finger off left hand.

Small scar over right eye.
Received 8/5/86
Paroled 1901

THIS TABLET ERECTED
IN MEMORY OF
ISRAEL SWAN
GEORGE NOON
FRANK MILLER
JAMES HUMPHREYS
WILSON BELL
WHO WERE MURDERED ON THIS SPOT
EARLY IN THE YEAR 1874
WHILE PIONEERING
THE MINERAL RESOURCES
OF THE SAN JUAN COUNTRY

Pioneer Memorial Tablet   Erected Aug. 1, 1928   1953 Photo

37

YOU ARE CORDIALLY INVITED TO BE PRESENT
AT THE

DEDICATION EXERCISES
OF THE

Pioneer Memorial Tablet

TO BE

CONDUCTED AT THE SITE OF THE GRAVES OF THE
PACKER VICTIMS, TWO MILES SOUTH OF
LAKE CITY, COLORADO

WEDNESDAY, AUGUST FIRST
NINETEEN HUNDRED TWENTY-EIGHT
AT ELEVEN O'CLOCK A. M.

THE PIONEER MEMORIAL TABLET

The Pioneer Memorial Tablet to be unveiled
on August 1st, on the site of the burial place
of the five men known as the Packer Victims,
was donated to the Ladies' Union Aid Society
of Lake City by Mr. M. B. Burke, prominent
mining man, of Denver and Lake City. The
graves of these men had remained almost alto-
gether neglected until a few years ago when
the Ladies' Union Aid Society undertook to
improve and appropriately mark the plot.
Since then a neat and substantial enclosure has
been built. With the unveiling of the Pioneer
Tablet, the work planned by the Society will
have been completed, the site of one of the
most terrible tragedies in Western American
history fitly marked, and the memory of its
victims preserved.

Program

Song—"America" ....Audience

Welcome Address..MRS. LUCY BEAM
President Ladies' Union Aid Society

Remarks..MR. M. B. BURKE
Donor of Tablet

Dedication Address....HON. JOHN C. BELL, of Montrose
Formerly of Lake City,
Prosecuting Attorney at
Trial of Alfred Packer.

Song ....MR. LYMAN E. READY

Remarks..MR. HERMAN MAYER
One of the participants
in the Court Proceed-
ings at the trial of Al-
fred Packer.

Remarks..HON. W. S. WHINNERY

Double Quartette—
MRS. CAROLYN WRIGHT, MISS LETA HUMPHREY,
MRS. PEARL McCLOUGHAN, MISS MARGARET
CUMMINGS; MESSRS. READY, MENDENHALL,
CUMMINGS, SHACKLETT.

Song—"Colorado" ....Audience

FISH FRY

A magnificent fish fry with all trimmings will be
served on the grounds for all in attendance, by Commit-
tees appointed by the Ladies' Union Aid Society.

38

SHORT SKETCH OF THE PACKER TRAGEDY

The Packer tragedy is one of the most famous in the crime history of the country. It is often referred to as the case of "Packer, the Man-eater." Briefly, the story is that, in the fall of 1873, a party of twenty-one prospectors outfitted at Provo, or Salt Lake, Utah, for the purpose of exploring the southwestern portion of Colorado, then in possession of the Ute Indians, for gold and silver, tales of the discovery of these precious metals having at that time been given large circulation. At the last minute one Alfred Packer was permitted to join the party as camp helper. At a point a short distance above where the present City of Montrose now stands, the party separated, six of them, the five to whose memory the Pioneer Tablet will be dedicated, and Packer, leaving the main party. What followed is a ghastly record from any viewpoint. In the spring of 1874 Packer appeared alone at the Los Pinos Indian Agency, where he fell in with Preston Nutter, one of the original Utah party. When questioned concerning the five companions who had started with him, Packer told a number of conflicting stories concerning their deaths from exposure and starvation and even of the killing of the five in succession and the eating of flesh from their bodies by the survivors. The bodies were later discovered a short distance from where they are now buried. Packer had been arrested at Saguache, but escaped and remained a fugitive until the spring of 1883, when he was captured at Wagonhound, near Fort Fetterman, Wyoming. He was brought to Lake City and tried for murder before M. B. Gerry, Esquire, District Judge. On April 13, 1883, he was found guilty and sentenced to be hanged on May 19 following. Because of legal technicalities he was granted a new trial and change of venue to Gunnison county. The second trial also resulted in his conviction, but instead of being sentenced to hang, Packer was given a sentence of forty years in the penitentiary. He was paroled in January, 1901, and died several years later, near Littleton, Colorado.

OFFICERS OF

THE LADIES' UNION AID SOCIETY
OF LAKE CITY, COLORADO

During the work of reclaiming, improving and providing the Tablet for the burial place of these Pioneers

1925

President................Mrs. Carolyn Wright
Vice President................Mrs. Edna Ramsey
Secretary-Treasurer.......Mrs. Alice Harkness

1926

President................Mrs. Helen S. Carey
Vice President................Mrs. Edna Ramsey
Secretary-Treasurer.......Mrs. Alice Harkness

1927

President................Mrs. Helen S. Carey
Vice President................Mrs. Edna Ramsey
Secretary-Treasurer.......Mrs. Edna Lampert

1928

President................Mrs. Lucy Beam
Vice President................Mrs. Alice Seibert
Secretary-Treasurer.......Mrs. Louise Heath

PIONEER MEMORIAL COMMITTEE

Mrs. Lillian F. Rawson, *Chairman*
Mrs. Alice Harkness
Mrs. Aileen Ready
Mrs. Evelyn Wilson

W. W. "Plug Hat" Anderson lef
shooting H. H. Tammen. Pol
Pry on right, Fred G. Bonfils c
the floor, wounded, Jan. 1.
1900. Anderson was tried 3 time
— April 19-28, 1900; Aug. 2-1
1901; Nov. 12-16, 1901. Th
first two were mistrials, the thir
trial resulted in a not guilty ve
dict. Bonfils was a devout Cath
olic, Anderson a very prominer
Mason.

Frederick G. Bonfils

Co-Founder of the Denver Post, Descendant of Napoleon, Promoter's Promoter, attended West Point, and was a brilliant conversationalist. Bon and Tam founded an unique bombastic, editorialistic, highly opinionated, rugged, personal, individualistic, vitalistic, rough-and-tumble brand of Journalism.

41

Harry H. Tammen

Co-Founder of the Denver Post, Ex-Bartender — Circus Fan and Owner
— Theatre and Novelty Tycoon. He told his employees, "Write what you
see and what you think. If a thing is horrible, tell why it is horrible, and
leave nothing to the imagination."

W. W. "Plug Hat" Anderson
— Athlete — Fearless Lawyer
Inveterate Peanut Eater
Prominent Mason

Polly Pry

Editor Dave Day wrote: "Polly Pry is possessed of a trait that always
stops the railroad train!"

L-R —John Kokas, Photographer; Carrie Lutz, Minta Smothers (wife), Clifford Smothers (husband), Peter Lenhart (mining promoter), Alferd Packer. Re-enacting the incident — "He came at me with an axe, and I had to shoot him through the belly!" Summer 1903, Clear Creek Canyon.

HOUSE JOINT MEMORIAL NO._____

(By Representatives Hart, Brotzman and Vanderhoof)

WHEREAS, It is fitting and proper that citizens who have made substantial and lasting contributions to the welfare of this great state should be suitably remembered by this Honorable Assembly; and

WHEREAS, The memory of one of Colorado's most distinguished citizens has not been properly preserved; and

WHEREAS, This man on or about March 1, 1873, in or near the County of Hinsdale, State of Colorado, rendered a service of lasting benefit to this State and to the United States; and

WHEREAS, The name of this celebrated and revered citizen, now deceased, was Alfred Packer; and

WHEREAS, The deed performed by this outstanding citizen was best described in the words of the Honorable Judge M. B. Gerry, Judge of the Seventh Judicial District for the County of Hinsdale, as follows:

"They was seven Democrats in Hinsdale County, but you, you voracious, man-eating beast, you ate five of them and I therefore order you hung by the neck till you are dead." and

WHEREAS, It is the sentiment of this Honorable Body that the stirring words of Judge Gerry be preserved for later generations of Colorado citizens; now, therefore,

It Is Hereby Resolved: That a 23-carat gold plaque be created at the State Capitol, commemorating this inspiring event and the great citizen responsible therefor, and that this plaque shall contain in raised letters the text of the remarks of Judge Gerry as read before.

In the second session of the 1952 House of Representatives, Speaker David Hamil, and Members Hart, Brotzman, and Vanderhoof, all Republicans, introduced, read and debated this memorial.

FOR FORTY YEARS.

uch is the Sentence Pronounced Upon Alfred Packer.

djudged by an Impartial Jury to Be Guilty as Charged.

ull Report of the Proceedings and Packer's Speech.

he Curtain at Last Falls Upon the Terrible Tragedy.

Guilty as Charged.

The Jury in the Packer case, after being at two and a half hours last evening, agreed pon a verdict and sent for Judge Harrison he thereupon convened court at 7:15 p. m. The Jury came in and handed a written erdict finding Packer guilty of voluntary anslaughter in each of the five cases.
Thos. C. Brown, attorney for the prisoner,

c me out: he of Saguache, tioned in the cleared him i [This is utter Packer pre neat watch he has been

A The court with citizens tence pronou word that he m Packer said he want he had prepa before the c nounced—M that was his to receive his

Court reco rison called "Mr. Pack up). "You of voluntary ments. If sentence is p so
Packer sai

Gunnison
Review Press
8-5-86

New York
Weekly Tribune
5-28-1859

JRDAY, MAY 28, 1859.   TW(

HORRIBLE FROM THE PLAINS.

THE RETURNING PIKE'S PEAKERS.

STARVATION and CANNIBALISM

MANY GRAVES ON THE ROUTE.

[Some additional intelligence from the unfortunate adventurers in the Pike's Peak country will be found on the second page of this paper]

[By Telegraph.]

ST. LOUIS, Tuesday, May 24, 1859.

The regular correspondent of *The Democrat*, writing from Denver City, on the 9th inst., recounts a most deplorable condition of things on the Plains. Many of the emigrants were dying of starvation, while others were subsisting on prickly pears and wild onions found along the road. The Stage Agent reports picking up a man named Blue, who was reduced to a skeleton from starvation. He had started with his two brothers. One of them died, and the remaining two ate his body. Another died, and he in turn was nearly devoured by the survivor. A man named Gibbs had reached the mines in a starving condition, and he expressed the opinion that his party, numbering nine, had all perished. Many graves are reported along the route, and much property had been abandoned and destroyed on the road.

The writer of the letter says that the departures from the mines are about equal to the arrivals.

About 500 returning emigrants reached St. Joseph on Saturday, all of whom confirm the previous accounts of the suffering and privations on the plains.

47

INDEX

Acknowledgments

We have been pursuing and collecting the Packer story for over 30 years. For help and cooperation in research we thank Ed Bemis, Don Brotzman, M.C., Harry Cole, Jim Davis. Lou Hart, Lorena Jones, Rial Lake, Alma B. Miller, John Vanderhoof, Warden Wayne Patterson, The Rocky Mountain News, The Denver Post, the Littleton Chamber of Commerce, and the Littleton Museum.

For the use of photographs, we are indebted to: Denver Post (1), Norman H. Dunham (1), Paul Gantt (4), Glenn L. Gebhardt (1), Numa James (1), Clifford Mills (1), Stella Pavich (1), Warden Wayne Patterson (2), Richard Ronzio (1), Dorothy Smith (1), Clifford Smothers (1), Dr. Philip Whiteley (1). The balance (45) are from the collection of Fred and Jo Mazzulla.

— Fred and Jo Mazzulla

Packer's Marker in the Littleton, Colo. Cemetery.

Let's not condemn poor Packer
  Nor crowd his soul with abuse
Though he hardly would merit approval,
  "Hunger" is valid excuse.

Politicians, historians and authors
  Have scoured his very last bone.
Yet out through the timeless forever
  His soul wanders on alone.

             — *Olive Nagel Porter*

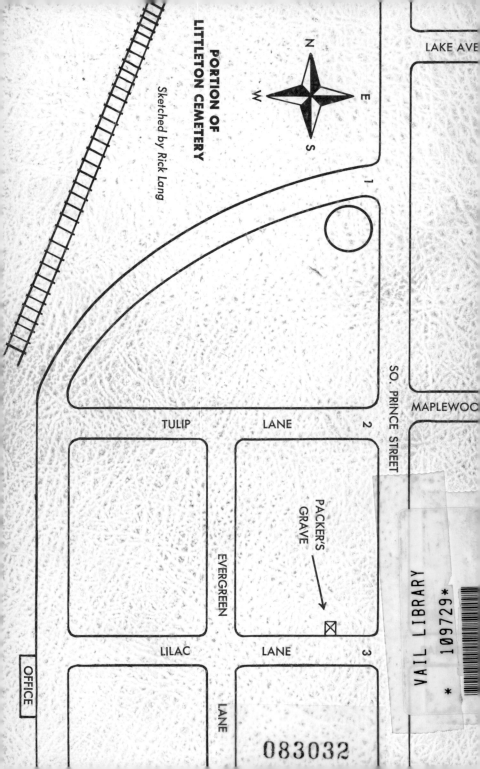

PORTION OF
LITTLETON CEMETERY

Sketched by Rick Lang

N
W   E
S

LAKE AVE

1

SO. PRINCE STREET

MAPLEWOO

TULIP   LANE   2

EVERGREEN

PACKER'S
GRAVE

LILAC   LANE   3

LANE

OFFICE